Inside Eye

BIG BUILDINGS OF THE MODERN WORLD

Written by
Dan Scott

CONTENTS

Inside Eye™ BIG BUILDINGS OF THE MODERN WORLD

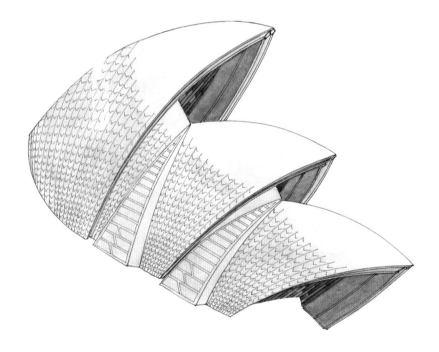

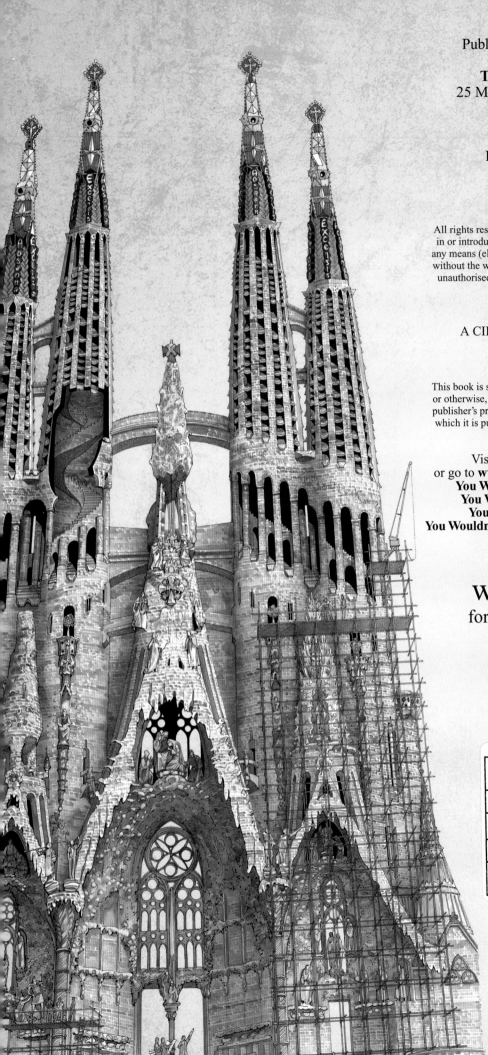

Published in Great Britain in MMXIV by
Book House, an imprint of
The Salariya Book Company Ltd
25 Marlborough Place, Brighton BN1 1UB
www.salariya.com
www.book-house.co.uk

PB ISBN-13: 978-1-909645-74-5

SALARIYA

A CIP catalogue record for this book is available
from the British Library.

Printed and bound in China.

Visit our website at **www.book-house.co.uk**
or go to **www.salariya.com** for **free** electronic versions of:
You Wouldn't Want to be an Egyptian Mummy!
You Wouldn't Want to be a Roman Gladiator!
You Wouldn't Want to be a Polar Explorer!
You Wouldn't Want to sail on a 19th-Century Whaling Ship

Visit
www.salariya.com
for our online catalogue and **free**
interactive web books.

PAPER FROM
SUSTAINABLE
FORESTS

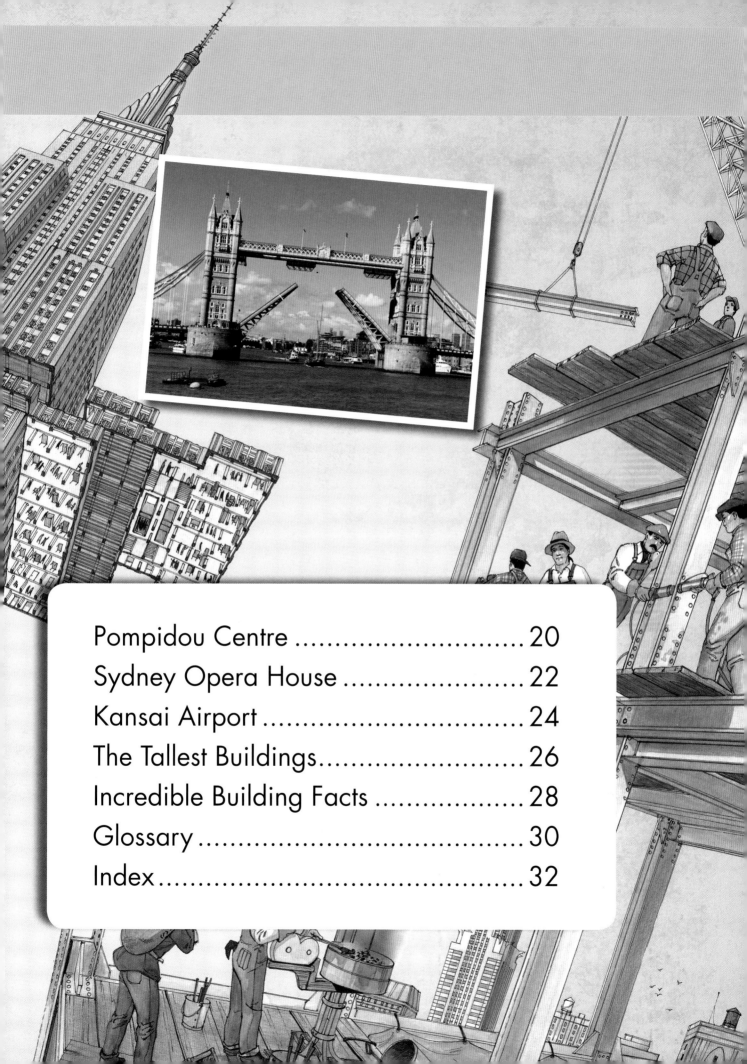

Super Structures

Our modern world is full of amazing big buildings. Some of these are churches, monuments and castles that survive from ancient times. However, in the past two centuries, this has expanded into an incredible, ever-increasing variety of huge structures: towers, bridges, skyscrapers, airports and arts centres. Each one reflects advances in engineering skills and technology that seem to know no bounds.

The Eiffel Tower is the most famous landmark in Paris.

The Sydney Opera House, in Australia, is one of the world's most impressive pieces of modern architecture.

6

The Sky's the Limit

For 4,000 years, the Great Pyramid at Giza in Egypt was the tallest building on Earth, at 147 m. Lincoln Cathedral overtook it in 1307, when a new spire raised the church's height to 160 m. That was the limit of technology until the Industrial Revolution of the nineteenth century brought the mass production of stronger materials such as cast iron and steel, which, alongside advanced engineering techniques, allowed buildings to soar higher. Before long, the 1 km height barrier will be broken, so who knows how far technology will take us?

The Royal Pavilion in Brighton has a remarkable architectural style inspired by the buildings seen by British travellers in India and China in the eighteenth and nineteenth centuries.

Inside Eye

In this book, we will look at incredible big buildings of all kinds, all around the world. We will discover who designed them, how they were built, what building materials were used and much more. And with an amazing 'inside eye' and stunning cutaway illustrations, we will show you exactly what each building looks like – from the inside out.

Royal Pavilion

In 1786, George, Prince of Wales, later to become Great Britain's King George IV, rented a farmhouse in Brighton. He loved the informality of the seaside resort, but the farmhouse did not suit his taste for luxury. The prince then embarked on 35 years of building works that combined his exuberant tastes with the skills of the architect John Nash, and the interior designers Frederick Crace and Robert Jones, to transform the modest farmhouse into an extraordinary oriental fantasy.

The Royal Pavilion's tent-like roofs were originally covered in mastic, a type of cement. However, the roofs leaked so they were replaced with copper coverings in 1827.

Balcony

Tent-like roof

The Great Kitchen

Skylight

Iron support

Elaborate Design

The Banqueting Room is the most elaborate example of the Pavilion's Chinese-style interiors. Nine chandeliers in the shape of lotus flowers light the room, and hundreds of plaster cockleshells cover the gilded, domed ceiling.

Antonin Carême, the greatest chef of his day and the inventor of crème caramel, became the chef at the Royal Pavilion in 1817. His meals were always elaborate – one menu listed 112 dishes.

Lotus leaf chandelier

Minaret

Dream Kitchen

For the early nineteenth century, the Great Kitchen of the Royal Pavilion had every modern convenience. The cooks had hot and cold running water and numerous ovens for stewing, roasting and baking. The central table was heated by steam running through concealed pipes. The roasting spit rotated automatically, powered by the rising heat of the fire. Copper canopies over the ovens carried away excess water vapour.

Prince of Pleasure

George, Prince of Wales, was born in 1762. He became Prince Regent in 1811 when his father, George III, grew too ill to rule. In 1820, the Prince finally succeeded to the throne but died 10 years later.

The Royal Pavilion is remarkable not only in appearance, but also in construction. Nash embraced the most advanced technology. Cast iron was a new building material, and Nash used it for the supports and framework of the Indian-style domes and minarets, and even to create delicate imitation bamboo staircases.

Statue of Liberty

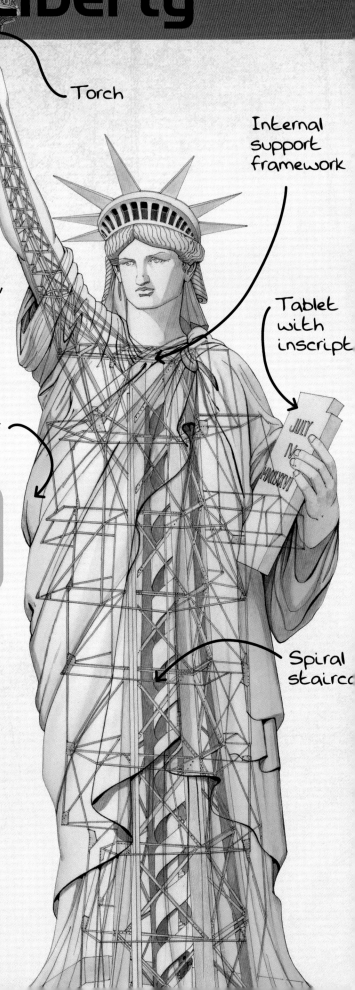

Torch

Internal support framework

Tablet with inscript

Copper outer covering

Spiral stairca

The most famous of American landmarks, the Statue of Liberty was the creation of a group of Frenchmen, including the sculptor Frédéric Auguste Bartholdi. They intended for the statue to celebrate the 100th anniversary of American independence from Great Britain. In 1886, 10 years after the anniversary, the Statue of Liberty was finally erected in New York Harbour, a gift from the people of France to the people of the United States.

Over the years, chemical reactions with the air have turned the copper structure green.

Metal Miracle

Building the Statue of Liberty was an enormous feat of technical engineering. The statue rises to a height of 93 m and weighs 204 tonnes. It is a hollow structure held up by a complex framework of iron posts, bracing struts, bars and metal straps, all covered in 300 sheets of copper, each one only about 3 mm thick. The iron bars are flexible, allowing Liberty's copper skin to expand and contract in the heat or cold and to absorb wind movement.

Liberty's hand is 5 m in length. The original torch was replaced in 1984 with a new copper torch covered in gold leaf.

Big Hand

By 1876, the 100th anniversary of American independence, the statue was far from finished. As a token gift, Liberty's hand, holding the torch, was sent to an exhibition in Philadelphia and then displayed in New York, before returning to France for completion. Eventually, the statue was shipped to New York in 210 crates and was pieced together on Bedloe Island – later renamed Liberty Island.

The seven spikes on Liberty's crown represent the seven continents and seven oceans of the world. Her face is 3 m wide and each eye is 0.8 m wide.

Starting Small

Before deciding on a final design for the Statue of Liberty, Bartholdi made several terracotta models. He drew on ancient Roman symbolism of Liberty as a woman, and his figures held aloft the light of truth.

Eiffel Tower

The Eiffel Tower formed the entrance to the Paris Exhibition of 1889, held to celebrate the 100th anniversary of the French Revolution. The engineer and designer, Alexandre-Gustave Eiffel, wanted to use the engineering skills and materials of the industrial age to erect the world's tallest building. The tower was 300 m high and was meant to last for 20 years as a temporary attraction – today, it is still the most famous landmark in Paris.

Third platform

Iron Wonder

The Eiffel Tower became the marvel of its day. It took a team of 50 engineers and a workforce of 230 men just over two years to build, using 18,038 wrought-iron components, held together by 2.5 million rivets. The splayed legs and open lattice-work of the 9,000-tonne structure allow wind to pass through, which means the tower can withstand the strongest of gales.

On a hot summer's day, the tower becomes slightly taller, with the metal expanding by as much as 17 cm.

Magician of Metal

When he began work on the Eiffel Tower, Alexandre-Gustave Eiffel had already built numerous bridges, domes and roofs throughout the world, using iron and steel. He designed the huge locks for the Panama Canal, as well as the framework of the Statue of Liberty.

First platform

Second platform

wrought-iron lattice-work

The full ascent to the top of the tower in the lifts took just 7 minutes, and 2,350 passengers could be carried to the top every hour.

Taking the Lift

When the tower was built, there were four double-decker glass-encased lifts up to the first platform, which had large restaurants, a 250-seat theatre and other facilities. Two more lifts ran to the second platform. Another lift then carried passengers to the top, where up to 800 people per day could enjoy panoramic views of Paris.

In 1959, a radio antenna was placed on the top of the tower, raising its height to 324 m.

Tower Bridge

In 1885, the British Parliament decreed that a new bridge should be built across the River Thames – the last crossing before the river reaches the North Sea. There were two big challenges. The bridge had to blend in with the Norman architecture of the nearby Tower of London, and it had to allow tall-masted ships to pass through. The Victorian designers of Tower Bridge, as it became known, found ingenious solutions.

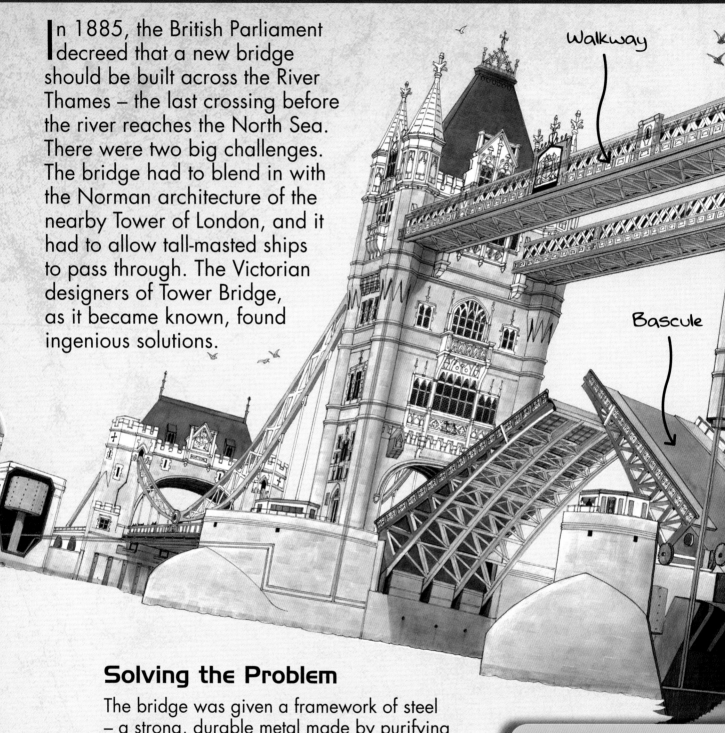

Walkway

Bascule

Solving the Problem

The bridge was given a framework of steel – a strong, durable metal made by purifying iron. On top of this framework, stone cladding and elaborate decoration were added to give the bridge a medieval style. Between the towers of the bridge were two central bascules, or specially balanced drawbridges, that could be raised by hydraulic engines to create enough space for the largest of ships to pass through.

The steel framework for the towers was faced with grey granite and Portland stone (a type of limestone) and backed with brick.

14

Each bascule weighed about 1,200 tonnes and could be fully raised in 60 seconds.

Brilliant Engineering

The hydraulic system was simple but a masterpiece of design. A boiler supplied steam to the pumping engine, which pumped water under pressure to six 100-tonne cylinders, called accumulators. These, in turn, sent high-pressure water along pipes to machines in the towers that turned a shaft with cogwheels at each end. The cogwheels then engaged with the teeth of huge quadrants, or quarter circles, which raised or lowered the bascules.

Cogwheel

Tower Bridge had four coal-burning, double-furnace boilers, each about 10 m long and with a diameter of more than 2 m. They used up to about 20 tonnes of coal each week to raise and lower the bridge's enormous bascules.

Northern Genius

The wealthy industrialist and engineer William George Armstrong (1810 – 1900) invented the hydraulic system for Tower Bridge. His home, Cragside in Northumberland, was the first house in the world to be lit by hydroelectricity.

Empire State Building

In the early twentieth century, Manhattan Island in New York City was a booming financial district but with limited room for office space. The answer was to build upward. This was made possible by the development of steel framing to support buildings and the invention of the electric lift. The skyscraper was born. Completed in 1931, the Empire State Building was the tallest skyscraper for 40 years, at 380 m high.

More than 6,000 windo

10 million bricks

Reach for the Sky

No skyscraper has been built as quickly as the Empire State Building. Work began in January 1930, and the building was finished on 11 April 1931. About 3,000 workers laboured on the site daily, many of them Mohawk Indians, who had no fear of heights. At one stage, 14 of the 108 storeys went up in 10 days.

In 1972, the World Trade Center, 419 m high, overtook the Empire State Building as the world's tallest skyscraper. Its twin towers were destroyed in a terrorist attack in 2001.

A Medieval Manhattan

The thirteenth-century skyline of the Italian city of Bologna was similar to that of modern Manhattan. As many as 100 or more fortified towers, some nearly 100 m tall, protected the richest families when the city was at war.

Radio tower

Riveters were paid just $1.92 (£1.17) per hour, and were given a lunch of sandwiches and coffee for 40 cents (33p).

Sky Team

The steel frames of the Empire State Building were held together with rivets. Riveting gangs consisted of five men – the heater, the catcher, the bucker-up, the driver and the riveter. The heater heated a rivet and threw it to the catcher, who jammed it into a rivet hole. The bucker-up then held the red-hot rivet in place while the driver hammered it from the other side to fuse it to the beam. The riveter supervised the whole gang.

61,000 tonnes of steel framing

When it was completed in 1930, the Chrysler Building in New York, at 319 m high, was briefly the tallest skyscraper in the world. The top section is decorated with the Chrysler car logo and a frieze of silver-coloured hubcaps.

Sagrada Familia

The leaning towers, warped surfaces and strange and lavish decorations of the church of the Sagrada Familia in Barcelona, Spain, make it one of the most original buildings of the modern world. It is the work of one man – architect Antoni Gaudí, who, from 1883, drastically altered the original plan for the church. Gaudí lived to see only part of his masterpiece completed, and the Sagrada Familia is still unfinished.

Gateway of Love

Gaudí's plan for the church included 12 bell towers – four for each of the three faces of the building – to represent the 12 apostles. Only four bell towers, each 92 m high, have been built on the east side. Below the towers is the magnificent 'Portal of Love', encrusted with flowing shapes and natural forms such as carvings of seashells and plants.

Cypress tree

At the time of Gaudí's death in 1926, only three towers had been finished.

Portal of Love

Gaudí was fascinated by symbolism, shapes and surfaces, and looked to the ocean, plants and rock formations for his inspiration.

Big Plans

The main body of the church, called the nave, is 100 m long. Above this, Gaudí planned to build even taller towers, as high as 170 m, around a central tower that represented Christ. Although work on the Sagrada Familia has continued for more than 130 years, the church that Gaudí envisaged will still take decades to complete. When it is finished, the Sagrada Familia is likely to be the biggest church in the world.

This is what the Sagrada Familia would look like if it had been finished. The areas in pink are not yet completed.

Wingless angel

Complete Original

Antoni Gaudí (1852 – 1926) was only 31 years old when he started work on the Sagrada Familia. He was already well known for his extraordinary buildings, which included influences from India, Persia and Japan, as well as the Moorish architecture of his own country.

Pompidou Centre

Between 1971 and 1977, a remarkable new building took shape in the Beaubourg area of Paris, France. Designed by an Englishman, Richard Rogers, and an Italian, Renzo Piano, the Pompidou Centre was one of the first 'high-tech' buildings. Its structural fabric and services, such as ventilation shafts and lifts, are revealed and boldly displayed on the outside of the building.

Cooling tower

Escalators run in transparent tubes on one side of the building, making their way past open viewing platforms.

Escalator

Big on the Inside

When the Pompidou Centre opened in 1977, about 2,000 people a day were expected to visit it. However, the Centre soon attracted 20,000 visitors daily. With all the building's functionality moved to the exterior, the architects were able to design large areas of open space inside for art galleries, a library and a music workshop. Each floor is the size of two football pitches.

The exterior colours of the Pompidou Centre each signify a different kind of mechanical function or service – blue for air-conditioning, yellow for electrics, green for water and red for escalators and lifts.

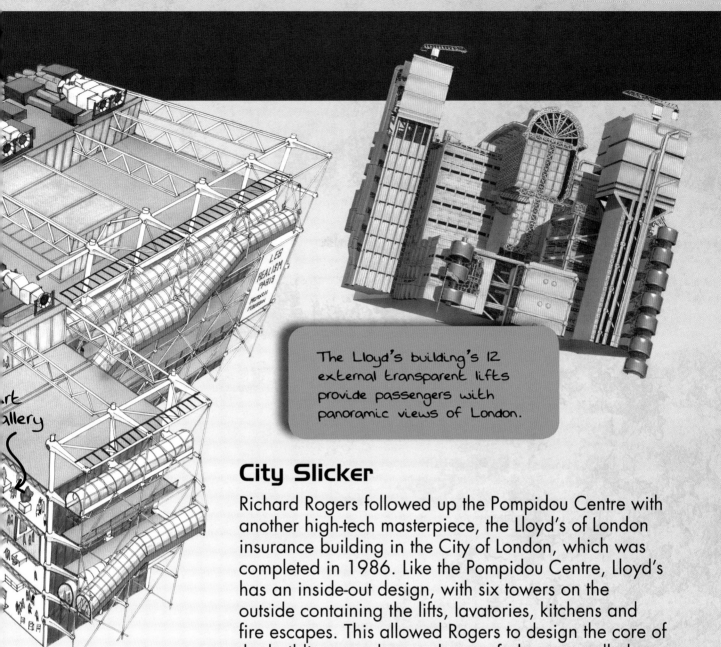

Gallery

Main entrance

The Lloyd's building's 12 external transparent lifts provide passengers with panoramic views of London.

City Slicker

Richard Rogers followed up the Pompidou Centre with another high-tech masterpiece, the Lloyd's of London insurance building in the City of London, which was completed in 1986. Like the Pompidou Centre, Lloyd's has an inside-out design, with six towers on the outside containing the lifts, lavatories, kitchens and fire escapes. This allowed Rogers to design the core of the building as a huge, glass-roofed space, called an atrium, that uses the full height of the structure.

The Lloyd's Bell

Lloyd's of London dates back to the seventeenth century and now operates from the vast trading room created by Richard Rogers. It contains the Lutine Bell, rescued from the ship *HMS Lutine*, which sank in 1799. The bell is rung whenever there is an important announcement.

Sydney Opera House

In 1955, the government of New South Wales, Australia, launched a competition to design a national opera house to be built in the state capital, Sydney. The winner was a little-known Danish architect, Jørn Utzon. His shell design for the Sydney Opera House, completed in 1973, has made it one of the most distinctive buildings in the world.

Collecting Shells

Work began in 1959. A deep, flat platform was built, jutting out into Sydney Harbour. Next, the sail-like shells, the tallest of which rises more than 67 m, were constructed from a series of concrete ribs strengthened by steel cables. This material, called reinforced concrete, could bend and stretch in the heat and allowed the architects to create daring structures with curving walls and roofs.

Beneath the shells are six venues for music, theatre and exhibitions. The site includes restaurants, bars, a library, shops and 60 dressing rooms.

Organ loft

Recordi halls

Opera theatre lounge

Opera theatre

Ceramic tiles in two colours – white and matt beige – cover the shells. The square tiles measure 12 cm – small enough to wrap around the curved surface.

Firm Support

The shells that form the Sydney Opera House appear to be supported by only two legs. In fact, the large shells are linked to smaller ones facing in the opposite direction. The two shells form one unit, and because each shell touches the ground at two points, the whole unit rests on four legs.

Amber-coloured glass walls fill the open ends of the structure. They are made from 2,000 panes of more than 700 different shapes, varying in size from about 1 m by 1 m to 4 m by 2.5 m.

French Opera

The Opéra Bastille in Paris, France, is another modern opera house. It was designed by the Canadian-Uruguayan architect Carlos Ott and was completed in 1989. The building's huge cylindrical shapes help it to blend in with the older surroundings, while thousands of transparent glass panels create a dramatic entrance.

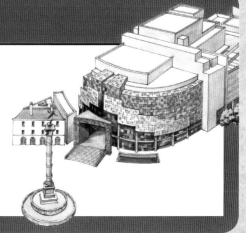

23

Kansai Airport

Kansai International Airport, situated on an artificial island 5 km off the east coast of Osaka Bay in Japan, is the world's first offshore airport. It was designed by Renzo Piano, one of the architects of the Pompidou Centre in Paris. Construction of the island began in 1987, and the airport opened in 1994. A second runway was opened in 2007 and around 17 million passengers now use Kansai each year.

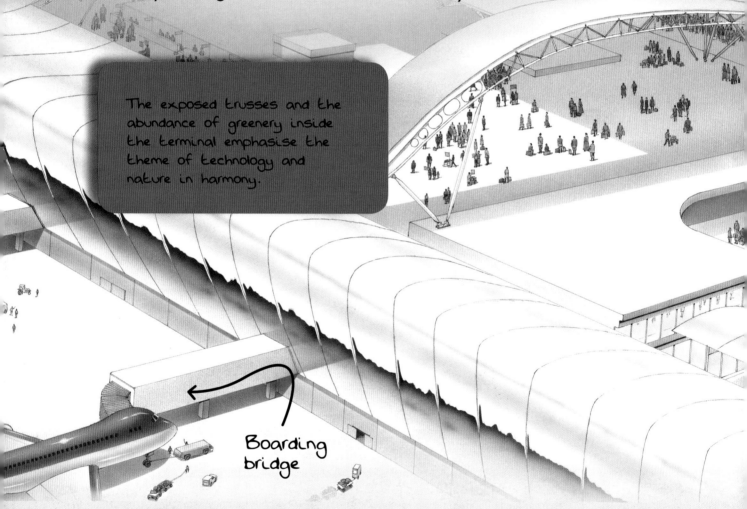

The exposed trusses and the abundance of greenery inside the terminal emphasise the theme of technology and nature in harmony.

Boarding bridge

Take to the Air

The main terminal's smooth flowing lines imitate those of an aircraft wing. The total length of the building is 1,660 m, making it the longest airport terminal in the world. The huge roof is supported in sections along its length by lightweight, tubular steel trusses. The roof span between the two leg supports at each end is over 80 m. Two three-storey wings to the north and south of the building house the aircraft gates.

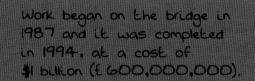

Work began on the bridge in 1987 and it was completed in 1994, at a cost of $1 billion (£600,000,000).

Wing-shaped extension

Bridge Over the Sea

A split-level bridge, 3.75 km long, carries motor vehicles and rail traffic from the mainland to the artificial island. The lower level carries two train lines and the upper level consists of two three-lane roadways. At the mainland end of the bridge, a new commercial and entertainment centre, Rinku Town, was developed on reclaimed land as part of the airport construction.

Passengers are whisked quickly to and from the aircraft gates on a driverless train called the Wing Shuttle. It is capable of carrying more than 44,000 people a day.

A New Island

The first step in making the artificial island was to erect a sea wall, using rocks and concrete. This was then filled to 30 m deep, with a layer of earth excavated from three nearby mountains. The weight of this landfill squeezed water out of the seabed, creating a secure foundation.

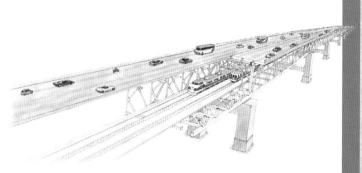

The Tallest Buildings

All cultures throughout the ages have wanted to build huge, impressive buildings. Structures such as the Egyptian pyramids, Greek temples and the cathedrals of medieval Europe still inspire admiration. However, the building materials and techniques of the modern world have freed architects from the constraints of traditional architecture and allowed them to push higher into the sky.

The skylines of the world's most famous cities are dominated by towering buildings. Imagine the skyline of a city made up of these skyscrapers alone!

Top Five Tallest Buildings

The world's top five tallest buildings are:

1. Burj Khalifa, Dubai: 830 m
2. Shanghai Tower, Shanghai, China: 632 m
3. Makkah Royal Clock Tower Hotel, Mecca: 601 m
4. One World Trade Center, New York City: 541 m
5. Taipei 101, Taipei, Taiwan: 509 m

Race to the Sky

Previously, a heavy stone structure could not be too tall or it would topple over. That all changed with the new technologies and materials of the industrial age, such as wrought iron and steel. This allowed Auguste-Gustave Eiffel to build a 300 m high tower in Paris, and led to New York City's own skyscraper race in the twentieth century. In the twenty-first century, it is now places in the Middle East and Far East, such as Dubai, Qatar, Malaysia and China, which are filling their cities with gigantic structures. In 2010, the Burj Khalifa skyscraper became the world's tallest building, at 830 m high. Before long, the race will break the seemingly impossible barrier of 1 km in height.

The Burj Khalifa (right) was designed by Skidmore, Owings and Merrill, the architects who also designed the Willis Tower in Chicago and the new One World Trade Center in New York City.

Incredible Facts

Dinner Is Served

A formal dinner in the Banqueting Room of the Royal Pavilion could last up to four hours and consist of 70 different dishes.

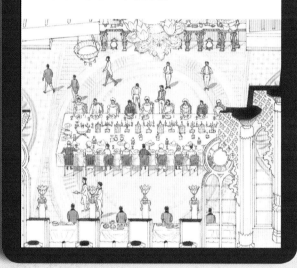

Head for Heights

Around 4 million people visit the Statue of Liberty each year. They have to climb 354 steps to reach the crown, where there are 25 viewing windows.

Puffed-out Dictator

When the Germans entered Paris during World War II, a mysterious fault in the Eiffel Tower lifts meant that Adolf Hitler was forced to climb the 1,792 steps to the top. When Paris was freed in 1944, it took only a quick turn of a screw to fix the fault!

Jumping Bus

In 1952, a London bus being driven over Tower Bridge by Albert Gunton had to leap from one bascule to the other when the bridge began to rise with the number 78 bus still on it.

Top Hits

The Empire State Building is struck by lightning an average of 25 times per year. In one storm, it was hit eight times in 24 minutes.

Tragic Accident

In 1926, Antoni Gaudí, the architect of the Sagrada Familia, was run over by a Barcelona tram. He is buried in a simple tomb in the crypt of the church.

High Accolade

In 2011, 25 years after completion, the Lloyd's of London building became the youngest-ever structure to receive Grade I listed status – the greatest protection a structure can be given in Britain.

Giant Building Kit

The roof of the Sydney Opera House is made up of 2,194 concrete sections, each weighing up to 15 tonnes, all held together by 350 km of steel cable.

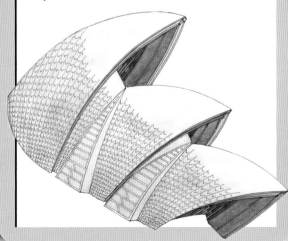

Architect the designer of a building.

Atrium a large internal space within a building, usually covered by glass.

Bascule a device that works like a see-saw. It is balanced so that when one end is lowered, the other is raised.

Beam a supportive section of a building's structure that usually runs from side to side.

Cast iron a mixture of iron and carbon produced by smelting ores. Cast iron is hard and brittle and cannot be shaped by hammering or rolling because it will break. It is poured, or cast, into moulds.

Concrete cement mixed with pebbles, crushed stone, sand and water.

Dome a rounded vault forming a roof.

Foundation the base of a structure, often below ground level, which carries the weight of a building.

Hydraulic operated by the movement of water though pipes or channels.

Iron a metallic element of great strength found throughout the Earth's crust in the form of ore.

Minaret a tall, slender tower inspired by Islamic architecture.

Pavilion an ornamental building used for entertainment.

Steel a metal made by reducing the carbon content of iron.

Terracotta unglazed, baked clay used for decoration or building.

Wrought iron a type of iron made by heating cast iron to make it finer. Wrought iron can be worked into many different shapes.